The Story of a Special Day
Volume 225

August
12

The 224th day of the year (225th in leap years).
There are 141 days remaining until the end of the year.

by Michael Dobson

Timespinner
Press

This book is also available in e-book form for Kindle, e-pub devices, and other formats from your favorite online booksellers.

For more information about the series, about us, or about your special day, please email us at editor@timespinnerpress.com.

Look for other volumes in *The Story of a Special Day,* coming often. See www.timespinnerpress.com for details and for the most recent information.

Table of Contents

Cover: Detail from *The Meeting of Antony and Cleopatra, 41 BC*, by Lawrence Alma-Tadena. Cleopatra committed suicide on August 12, 30 BCE — the **Event of the Day**.

Quote of the Day

"Being brilliant to look upon and to listen to, with the power to subjugate everyone, even a love-sated man already past his prime...she reposed in her beauty all her claims to the throne."

Roman historian Cassius Dio describing Cleopatra
Cleopatra died August 12, 30 BCE

Today in History

August 12

A contemporary bust of Cleopatra (Photo: Ángel M. Felicísimo)

Event of the Day
August 12, 30 BCE —
The Death of Cleopatra

On August 12, 30 BCE*, Cleopatra, legendary ruler of Egypt and lover of both Julius Caesar and Mark Antony, died, most probably by suicide, though whether it was by means of a snake bite or through poison has been debated by historians for many centuries.

Although she was briefly survived as pharaoh by her son Caesarion, she was the last actual ruler of Ptolemaic Egypt before it was turned into a province of the Roman Empire.

A *cartouche* showing the name of Cleopatra VII in Egyptian hieroglyphs

---

* For the meaning and use of "BCE," see the section "On Names and Dates."

The Early Life of Cleopatra

Although Cleopatra was Pharaoh of Egypt, she was not herself Egyptian, but rather Macedonian Greek. Following the death of Alexander the Great, her ancestor Ptolemy, one of Alexander's generals, took over Egypt. His descendants would rule the kingdom for the next 275 years.

Males of the Ptolemaic dynasty were usually named Ptolemy; females were named either Cleopatra, Berenice, or Arsinoë. The Cleopatra of our story was officially named Cleopatra VII Philopator (Κλεοπάτρα Φιλοπάτωρ). Her father, Ptolemy XII Auletes ("flute player"), known as an ineffectual and weak ruler, appointed her as his co-ruler at the age of 14, following his return to power after having been deposed and exiled. Four years later, he died, leaving the 18-year old Cleopatra as joint ruler with her 10-year old brother Ptolemy XIII. The siblings had a falling out, and the young Ptolemy forced her from the throne and drove her into exile.

Caesar and Cleopatra

Meanwhile, Rome had degenerated into civil war. Gaius Julius Caesar, who had declared himself dictator, was pursuing his former ally Pompey the Great. Defeated in battle, Pompey fled to Egypt to seek sanctuary, but the 13-year old Ptolemy had him beheaded instead, hoping to ingratiate himself with Caesar.

Cleopatra and Caesar, by Jean-Léon Gérôme

Claudette Colbert in *Cleopatra* (1934)

Unfortunately for Ptolemy, Caesar was not pleased. Regardless of the current conflict, Pompey was still a Roman consul, as well as the widower of Caesar's daughter Julia. In revenge, Caesar seized the city of Alexandria.

Cleopatra saw her opportunity. She snuck into the palace rolled up in a carpet. Caesar was evidently quite impressed, and restored her to the throne. He also took her as his mistress (she was 21; he was 52), and together they had a son, Ptolemy Caesar, nicknamed "Caesarion," or "little Caesar."

It's well known that Egyptian pharaohs typically married their brothers or sisters, but this was not actually required. Instead, because the pharaohs of Egypt were officially considered to be gods, they were required to mate with other gods, and there weren't a lot to choose from. Caesar, however, was a member of the Julii family, who claimed descent from Aeneas, a prince of Troy and mythological hero of Rome, whose story is told in Virgil's *Aeneid*. Aeneas's mother, according to the story, was the goddess Venus, and therefore Caesar was officially considered to be of divine blood. This made him a suitable consort for Cleopatra.

Following their victory, Cleopatra and Caesar traveled down the Nile in the royal barge, with 400 ships accompanying them. Cleopatra followed Caesar back to Rome, though as a foreign ruler she was not permitted to come into the city herself. She was living outside Rome when Caesar was assassinated in 44 BCE.

Cleopatra wanted Caesar to name her son as his heir, but Caesar had refused, naming his nephew Octavian (later known as Augustus) instead. On her return to Egypt, she made Caesarion her co-ruler and successor.

Antony and Cleopatra

Cleopatra was not the only one upset when Caesar made Octavian his heir. Mark Antony, one of Caesar's top generals as well as a relative of his, thought he should have been Caesar's heir. He was, after all, Caesar's second-in-command. However, Mark Antony didn't have the power to take control, so ended up in an uneasy alliance with Octavian and Marcus Aemilius Lepidus, known to history as the Second Triumvirate. Together, they defeated the forces of Caesar's assassins Cassius and Brutus.

Sarah Bernhardt in an 1891 stage production of *Antony and Cleopatra* (Photo: Napoleon Sarony)

The Battle of Actium

In the aftermath, Mark Antony became ruler of all of Rome's eastern provinces as well as of Gaul. Egypt now fell under his control, and in October of 41 BCE, Cleopatra visited Antony. The two began a relationship. (As a relative of Caesar's, Mark Antony was also considered to have divine blood.)

While Mark Antony was the best known and most powerful triumvir, Octavian was by far the better politician. He condemned Antony for "going native" with his relationship with Cleopatra, and in particular protested Antony's support of Caesarion, whose relationship to Caesar was a particular threat to Octavian's legitimacy. Soon, a propaganda war turned into a real war, known as the Final War of the Roman Republic. It would come to its conclusion near the promontory of Actium in what is now Greece.

The Battle of Actium

The conflict between Octavian and Antony came to a head in one of the most famous naval battles in history, the Battle of Actium.

On the morning of September 2, 31 BCE. Octavian's fleet of 250 warships challenged more than 500 of Antony's, about half large war galleys with towers packed with armed men. Although powerful, Antony's larger ships were less maneuverable.

Before the battle, one of Antony's generals had defected, providing Agrippa with Antony's battle plans. Armed with that knowledge, Agrippa waited until Antony was forced to attack. The battle raged throughout the day, when Antony misread a signal and concluded that his fleet was retreating in panic.

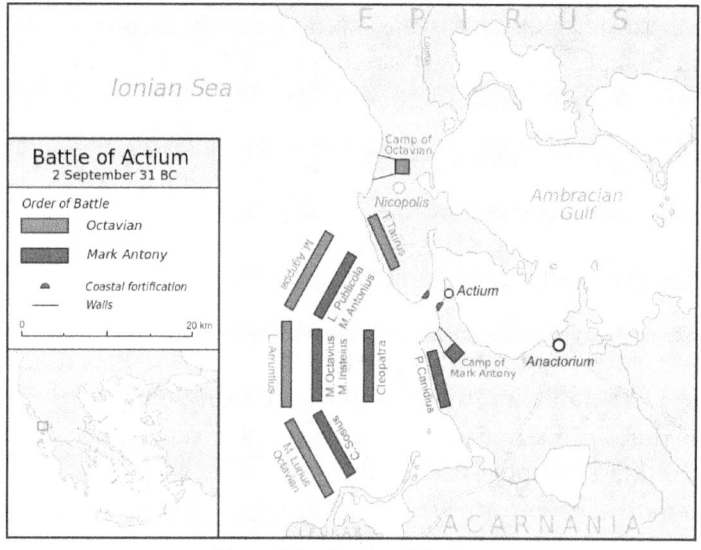

Map of the Battle of Actium

The Death of Cleopatra

As Octavian's forces moved toward Egypt, Cleopatra realized that for her as well, the end had come. If she stayed alive, she would be captured and taken to Rome, where she would be paraded in Octavian's triumph before being exiled or killed.

Ancient sources state that she had an Egyptian cobra (asp) bite her; more modern sources suggest that she was possibly murdered or that she drank poison. A few sources suggest that Octavian did manage to capture her, and that she committed suicide while in his captivity. However, it was the story of Cleopatra and the asp that became famous in history. When Octavian did finally celebrate his triumph in Rome, his parade included an effigy of Cleopatra with an asp clinging to it.

She was 39 years old when she died.

Her co-ruler and son Caesarion was proclaimed sole pharaoh by the Egyptians, but his rule only lasted 11 days. He was captured and killed, presumably on the direct orders of Octavian, who had been advised, "It is bad to have too many Caesars." Thus ended the line of Egyptian pharaohs.

Caesarion was the only threat to Octavian. Cleopatra's three children by Mark Antony were taken back to rome, where Antony's wife took them in. Egypt as an independent nation ceased to exist, and became instead the Roman province of Aegyptus.

Cleopatra in History and Popular Culture

Cleopatra was regarded as a great beauty. In his *Life of Antony*, Plutarch writes that 'judging by the proofs...of the effect of her beauty...she had hopes that she would more easily bring Antony to her feet. For Caesar and Pompey had known her when she was still a girl and inexperienced in affairs, but she was going to visit Antony at the very time when women have the most brilliant beauty."

However, it's not her beauty, but her wit, charm, and "sweetness in the tones of her voice" that Plutarch says was at the heart of her appeal. She was also known for her intellect; according to Plutarch, she could speak at least nine languages.

In popular culture, Cleopatra is by far the most famous of all Egyptian pharaohs. Playwrights from Shakespeare to George Bernard Shaw have been enthralled by her story; there have been operas, at least 20 films, and several TV series about her life. Her life, and especially her death, have been the subject of numerous paintings.

She is considered one of the great *femme fatales* of history, but that is selling her short. She managed to navigate some of the most dangerous political waters for much of her life, using all the weapons available to her. Although she could not in the end prevent Rome's conquest of Egypt, she fought valiantly and effectively throughout her life.

Cleopatra, by Michelangelo

Advertisement for Singer sewing machines, circa 1900

What Happened on August 12?

From the creation of great works of engineering and art, to devastating wars and natural disasters, thousands of years of history have left their mark on each and every day of the year. Here are some important events that occurred on August 12. (Items with a photo or illustration are boxed.)

1099 — In the Battle of Ascalon, Crusader army defeats and drives off forces from the Fatimid Caliphate to secure the safety of Jerusalem in the **last action of the First Crusade.**

1765 — With the signing of the Treaty of Allahabad between the Mughal Emperor and the East India Company, **British rule in India** begins.

1851 — Inventor Isaac Singer receives a patent for the **first practical sewing machine**.

1883 — The last **quagga,** a type of zebra, dies in captivity. Its name comes from its call, which sounds like "kwa-ha-ha." *(Photo next page.)*

1898 — The nominally independent **Republic of Hawai'i ceases to exist** when it is formally annexed by the United States. It had replaced the Kingdom of Hawaii in 1893.

1960 — The **first successful American communications satellite**, Echo 1A, is launched by NASA. It is expected to last until 1963 or 1964, but instead survives until 1968.

1981 — The **first IBM Personal Computer**, a major development in microcomputers, goes on the market.

1990 — The **largest and best-preserved example of** *Tyrannosaurus rex*, **"Sue,"** is discovered in South Dakota.

A quagga in the Regent's Park Zoo, London (Photo: Frederick York, 1870, courtesy Biodiversity Heritage Library)

The original IBM 5150 Personal Computer (Photo: Ruben de Rijcke, CC BY-SA 3.0)

Quote of the Day

"You know how to whistle, don't you, Steve? You just put your lips together — and blow."

Lauren Bacall to Humphrey Bogart
in the 1944 film *To Have and Have Not*
Bacall died August 12, 2014

Births
and
Deaths

August 12

Lauren Bacall (left), with Humphrey Bogart in the 1945 film *To Have and Have Not*. Bacall died August 12, 2014.

Notable August 12 People

With the current world population at about seven billion people, on average about 19 million people also celebrate their birthdays on August 12 — and that isn't counting millions and millions who came before! No matter when you were born, you share your birthday with many special people whose accomplishments (and occasionally embarrassments) have been noted as part of history.

In this section, you'll meet fascinating people who share your birthday. They're organized by what they're famous for, and then in reverse chronological order from most recent to earliest. Those who are shown in photographs or artwork have a box around them. We don't have photos of everyone, so please forgive us if your favorite person is missing.

Some of these people you've heard of, others will be new to you, but they all make up an important part of the reason that August 12 is a truly special day!

Tsarevich Alexei and his father Tsar Nicholas II

Who Was Born on August 12?

Art and Illustration

Tedd Pierce, writer for the Warner Brothers animation studio, credited as the inspiration for the cartoon character Pepé Le Pew. *(1906)*

Business

George Soros, investor and political activist known as "the man who broke the Bank of England." *(1930)*

Diamond Jim Brady, American businessman, financier, and philanthropist. *(1856)*

Government and Politics

Alexei Nikolaevich, Tsarevich of Russia (Алексей Никола́евич), last Romanov heir to the Russian throne, murdered along with his family during the Bolshevik Revolution. *(1904 [O.S†. July 31])*

Klara Hitler, mother of Adolf Hitler. *(1860)*

---

† Russia converted from the Julian "Old Style" calendar to the Gregorian "New Style" calendar later than the rest of Europe, July 31 in "Old Style" converts to August 12 "New Style." See "On Names and Dates" for more.

Journalism and Literature

William Goldman, novelist and screenwriter known for *Butch Cassidy and the Sundance Kid, Marathon Man,* and *The Princess Bride. (1931)*

Norris and Ross McWhirter, twin brothers best known as the founder of *Guinness World Records. (1925)*

Mary Roberts Rinehart, mystery writer sometimes called the "American Agatha Christie," credited with originating the phrase "The butler did it." *(1876)*

Edith Hamilton, classicist and historian known for her books *The Greek Way, The Roman Way,* and *Mythology. (1867)*

Jacinto Benavente, Spanish dramatist who wrote over 170 works; won the 1922 Nobel Prize in Literature. *(1866)*

Music and Dance

Sir Mix-a-Lot, rapper whose best known hit was the 1991 single "Baby Got Back." *(1963)*

Mark Knopfler, lead singer, guitarist, and songwriter for the band Dire Straits. *(1949)*

Buck Owens, country music star, pioneered the "Bakersfield sound," co-hosted the TV series *Hee Haw,* member of the Country Music Hall of Fame. *(1929)*

Buck Owens, Lisa Todd, and Roy Clark from *Hee Haw*

Porter Wagoner, country music star known as "Mr. Grand Ole Opry," member of the Country Music Hall of Fame. *(1927)*

Michael Kidd, stage and film choreographer whose best known works include the dances in *Seven Brides for Seven Brothers* and *The Band Wagon.* (1915)

Katharine Lee Bates, songwriter known for writing the lyrics to "America the Beautiful" and for popularizing "Mrs. Santa Claus "*(1859)*

Religion

Father Michael J. McGivney, American priest who founded the Knights of Columbus. *(1852)*

Helena Blavatsky (Еле́на Блава́тская), Russian occultist who co-founded the Theosophical Society. *(1831 [O.S.‡ July 31])*

Science and Technology

Vikram Sarabhai, regarded as the father of India's space program. *(1919)*

Erwin Schrödinger, received the 1933 Nobel Prize in Physics for his Schrödinger equation, best known for his "Schrödinger's Cat" thought experiment. *(1887)*

Sports

Cindy Klassen, Canadian speed skater who received five medals at the 2006 Winter Olympics. *(1979)*

---

‡Russia converted from the Julian "Old Style" calendar to the Gregorian "New Style" calendar later than the rest of Europe, July 31 in "Old Style" converts to August 12 "New Style." See "On Names and Dates" for more.

Pete Sampras, tennis player ranked World No. 1, often listed as one of the greatest tennis players of all time. *(1971)*

Christy Mathewson, pitcher who played 17 seasons with the New York Giants, considered one of the top pitchers in baseball history, one of the first five players elected to the Baseball Hall of Fame. *(1880)*

Christy Mathewson

Stage and Screen

Dominique Swain, actress best known for playing the title role in the 1997 film version of *Lolita. (1980)*

Maggie Lawson, actress known for playing Detective O'Hara in the TV comedy-mystery series *Psych. (1980)*

Casey Affleck, member of the Affleck family of actors whose films include *To Die For, Good Will Hunting,* and the *Ocean's* trilogy. (1975)

Yvette Nicole Brown, actress best known as Shirley from the TV sitcom *Community. (1971)*

Bruce Greenwood, actor known for roles in such films as *Thirteen Days, Star Trek* (2009), and *Star Trek Into Darkness. (1956)*

George Hamilton, well-known film and television actor. *(1939)*

John Cazale, actor best known for playing Fredo in the *Godfather* films. *(1935)*

John Derek, actor and director known for developing the careers of his second wife, Ursula Andress, and of his fourth wife, Bo Derek. *(1926)*

Cantinflas (Mario Moreno), Mexican comic actor who became an iconic figure in Latin America; won a Golden Globe for his role as Passepartout in the 1956 film *Around the World in 80 Days. (1911)*

Cantinflas (Mario Moreno) starring in the 1942 film *Los Tres Mosqueteros (The Three Musketeers)*

Jane Wyatt, actress best known for playing the mother on the TV series *Father Knows Best,* and the mother of Spock on the original *Star Trek. (1910)*

Jane Wyatt (right), with Leonard Nimoy (center) and Mark Lenard (left), from the *Star Trek* episode "Journey to Babel."

Alfred Lunt, stage director and actor best known for his long partnership with his actress wife Lynn Fontanne; namesake of Broadway's Lunt-Fontanne Theatre. *(1892)*

Cecil B. DeMille, founding father of the motion picture industry and the most commercially successful producer-director in cinematic history. His famous films include *The Ten Commandments, The Greatest Show on Earth,* and *Cleopatra. (1881)*

Cecil B. De Mille director credit slide from the 1918 silent film *We Can't Have Everything*

George Stephenson with his first steam locomotive, "The Rocket,"
Liverpool and Manchester Railway, 1829.

Who Died on August 12?

Art and Illustration

Joe Kubert, comic book artist who founded The Kubert School, which produced numerous well-known comics artists; member of the Jack Kirby Hall of Fame and the Will Eisner Comic Book Hall of Fame. *(2012)*

Jean-Michel Basquiat, former graffiti artist whose neo-expressionist paintings are in many modern museum collections. *(1988)*

Business and Technology

William Shockley, inventor and physicist whose breakthroughs in the development of transistors led to the development of the high-tech region known as "Silicon Valley," shared the 1956 Nobel Prize in Physics for his work. *(1989)*

Eliphalet Remington, inventor and businessman who designed the Remington rifle and founded the company E. Remington and Sons. *(1861)*

George Stephenson, "Father of Railways," engineer who built the first public inter-city railway line using steam locomotives. *(1848)*

Crime and Punishment

Matthew Hopkins, Witchfinder General during the English Civil War, responsible for more than 300 women being executed as witches. *(1647)*

MATTHEW HOPKINS,
OF MANNINGTREE, ESSEX,
THE CELEBRATED WITCH-FINDER.

Games and Sports

Wilhelm Steinitz, Austrian-American chess grandmaster and world champion, also known for his writings on chess theory. *(1900)*

Government and Politics

Lord Castlereagh, British foreign secretary during the Napoleonic wars, responsible for managing the anti-Napoleon coalition. *(1822)*

Journalism and Literature

Esther Forbes, novelist best known for her award-winning novel *Johnny Tremain*. *(1967)*

Ian Fleming, British naval intelligence officer who created the fictional spy James Bond. *(1964)*

Thomas Mann, German novelist famous for such works as *Buddenbrooks, Death in Venice,* and *The Magic Mountain*; received the 1929 Nobel Prize in Literature. *(1955)*

James Russell Lowell, American poet of the Romantic era. *(1891)*

William Blake, English poet and painter who wrote "The Tyger." *(1827)* *(Photo next page.)*

Military

Joseph P. Kennedy, Jr., bomber pilot killed on a secret mission during World War II, eldest brother of US President John F. Kennedy. *(1944)*

William Blake (self-portrait, 1802)

Music

Richie Hayward, drummer for the rock band Little Feat. *(2010)*

Les Paul, guitarist, songwriter, and inventor known for his work in developing the electric guitar, only person to be elected to both the Rock and Roll Hall of Fame and the National Inventors Hall of Fame. *(2009)*

John Cage, avant-garde composer best known for his 1952 composition *4'33"* and for his long association with choreographer Merce Cunningham. *(1992)*

John Cage (Photo: Rob Bogaerts)

Kyu Sakamoto (坂本 九), Japanese singer and actor who became the first Asian recording artist to have a *Billboard* No. 1 song in the US for his 1963 hit "Ue o Muite Arukō" ("Sukiyaki"). *(1985)*

Religion

Innocent XI, pope known as the "Savior of Hungary." *(1689)*

Science

Sir Godfrey Hounsfield, electrical engineer who shared the 1979 Nobel Prize for Physiology or Medicine for helping develop X-ray computed tomography, better known as the CT scan. *(2004)*

Sir Ernst Boris Chain, British biochemist who shared the 1945 Nobel Prize in Physiology or Medicine for his work on penicillin. *(1979)*

Karl Ziegler, German chemist, shared the 1963 Nobel Prize in Chemistry for his work on polymers. *(1973)*

Walter Rudolf Hess, Swiss physiologist who shared the 1949 Nobel Prize in Physiology or Medicine for mapping the areas of the brain that control internal organs. *(1973)*

James B. Sumner, American chemist who shared the 1946 Nobel Prize in Chemistry for his discovery that enzymes could be crystallized, proved that enzymes were proteins. *(1955)*

Sports

Enos Slaughter, baseball right fielder primarily for the St. Louis Cardinals, known for scoring the winning run of Game Seven of the 1946 World Series, member of the National Baseball Hall of Fame. *(2002)*

Stage and Screen

Lauren Bacall, actress known for such films as *To Have and Have Not, The Big Sleep, Key Largo,* and *How to Marry a Millionaire;* married to actor Humphrey Bogart. *(2014)* *(Photo page 18)*

Merv Griffin, gained fame with his 1950 hit "I've Got a Lovely Bunch of Coconuts," hosted his own eponymous syndicated talk show, and created and produced the game shows *Jeopardy!* and *Wheel of Fortune. (2007)*

Loretta Young, host of the long-running *The Loretta Young Show,* won the Best Actress Oscar for the 1947 film *The Farmer's Daughter. (2000)*

Henry Fonda, actor famous for such films as The Grapes of Wrath, Mister Roberts, 12 Angry Men, and On Golden Pond; father of actors Jane and Peter Fonda, and grandfather of actors Bridget Fonda and Troy Garity. *(1982)*

Anna Held, Broadway performer and singer best known for her relationship with impressario Florenz Ziegfeld, dramatized in the 1936 film *The Great Ziegfeld. (1918)*

Anna Held

August, from *Labors of the Months* by Simon Bening

Quote of the Day

"If the doors of perception were cleansed, everything would appear to man as it is: infinite."

William Blake, poet
died August 12, 1827

Holidays Around the World

August 12

"The Grouse Shoot," by Heywood Hardy — for **Glorious Twelfth**

Holidays Around the World

If you're looking for a reason to take your special day off, you should know that every single day is a holiday somewhere in the world! Here's some of what you can celebrate on August 12!

General Events

Air Force Day *(Russia)*. Russian Air Force Day (День Военно-воздушных сил) honors active duty, reserve, and retired members of that branch of the Russian military.

Glorious Twelfth *(Great Britain and Northern Ireland)*. Glorious Twelfth is a popular nickname for the traditional start of the shooting season for red grouse. *(If August 12 falls on a Sunday, it takes place on Monday, August 13, instead.)*

International Youth Day *(United Nations)*. To draw attention to youth issues worldwide, the United Nations observes International Youth Day on August 12.

Mother's Day/Queen's Birthday *(Thailand)*. Mother's Day in Thailand is celebrated on the birthday of Queen Dowager Sirikit, born in 1932.

World Elephant Day *(international)*. World Elephant Day is dedicated to the preservation and protection of the world's elephants.

Food Holidays

In the United States, almost every day of the year is dedicated to a particular food. (Some other countries do this also, but not every day.) Sponsored by manufacturers, retailers, farmers, or simply fans, these days are often proclaimed by the President, Congress, state governors, or mayors. Given that there are more different foods than days of the year, some days honor more than one kind of food!

August 12 is **National Julienne Fries Day**. What Americans call French fries, the English call "chips." They actually originated in Belgium, though potatoes came from the New World. The first serving of French fries in America is attributed to a diplomatic dinner hosted by Thomas Jefferson.

In addition, the entire month of August is used to celebrate numerous foods. Here's a list of what to eat in the month of August!

- National Catfish Month
- National Goat Cheese Month
- National Panini Month
- National Peach Month
- National Sandwich Month

Catfish, by Utagawa Kuniyoshi — for **National Catfish Month**

Honorary Months

Presidents, Congresses, and nations around the world issue proclamations recognizing particular months to honor certain causes. These events generally fall in August, though honorary months do come and go. Holidays established by states and nonprofit organizations are listed if verified. If not otherwise specified, all months are US. There is some variation from year to year; some celebratory months get added and others get dropped. Two places to get up to date information are the current edition of *Chase's Calendar of Events* or the website Brownielocks (www.brownielocks.com). Here are some honorary designations for August.

- American Adventures Month
- American Artists Appreciation Month
- American Indian Heritage Month
- Audio Appreciation Month
- Bystander Awareness Month
- Children's Eye Health and Safety Month
- Child Support Awareness Month
- National Children's Vision and Learning Month
- Digestive Tract Paralysis (DTP) Month
- Get Ready for Kindergarten Month
- Month of Philippine Languages (Philippines)
- National Back to School Month
- National Black Business Month
- National Breastfeeding Month
- National Immunization Awareness Month

A photograph from a nursery school operated for women working in the war effort, 1943. (Photo: Marjory Collins for the Farm Security Administration, Office of War Information) — for **Get Ready for Kindergarten Month.**

- National Lawn Games Month
- National Minority Donor Awareness Month
- National Water Quality Month
- Neurosurgery Outreach Month
- Psoriasis Awareness Month
- Spinal Muscular Atrophy Awareness Month
- What Will Be Your Legacy Month
- Win with Civility Month
- Family Meals Month
- Tomboy Tools Month

Moveable and Multi-Day Events

Some events take place over a specific week or time period. Start and finish dates may vary from year to year. Some events occur on different days each year (such as "fourth Saturday of a month"). These events sometimes take place on August 12.

Sunday on or closest to August 9 (August 7-12)

- National Peacekeepers' Day *(Canada)*

2nd Sunday (August 8-14)

- Children's Day *(Argentina, Chile, Uruguay)*
- Father's Day *(Brazil. Samoa)*
- Melon Day *(Turkmenistan)*
- Navy Day *(Bulgaria)*

2nd Monday (August 8-14)

- Heroes' Day *(Zimbabwe)*
- Father's Day *(Samoa)* *(Monday after the 2nd Sunday)*
- Victory Day *(Hawaii and Rhode Island)*

2nd Tuesday (August 8-14)

- Defence Forces Day *(Zimbabwe)*

2nd Saturday (August 8-14)
- Middle Child Day *(US)*
- National Bowling Day *(US)*
- Sports Day *(Russia)*

Religious Observances and Holidays

Sea Org Day *(Scientology)*. Members of the Scientology "Sea Organization" hold celebrations with rank and rating promotion ceremonies on this day.

Saint Days *(Christianity)*
Each day in the year is considered a feast day for one or more saints. They are somewhat different in western Christianity (Catholicism and many forms of Protestantism) and in eastern (Orthodox) Christianity. There are many others; this is a selection.

In *Western Christianity*, August 12 is the feast day of Saints Euplius, Herculanus of Brescia,.Jaenberht, Jane Frances de Chantal, and Pope Innocent XI.

In *Eastern Orthodox Christianity*, it is also the commemoration of Saints Sergius and Stephen, Gracilian and Felicissima, Cassian of Benevento, Eusebius of Milan, Molaise of Devenish, Muredach, Seigine, Porcarius, Jambert, Merewenna, and Ust.. (These are observed on July 30 by Orthodox churches that use the "Old Calendar[§].")

[§] For an explanation of the Old (Julian) Calendar and the New (Gregorian) Calendar, see "What Day of the Week is August 12?"

Just for Fun

Anybody can make up a holiday, and many people do! While none of these are officially recognized and some may come and go, here are a few more holidays for August 12.

- IBM PC Day

- Milkman Day

- National Garage Sale Day *(second Saturday)*

A milkman, by Gottfried Mind — for **Milkman Day**

August, by Joachim von Sandrart

Quote of the Day

"Make haste slowly."

Augustus, first emperor of Rome
and namesake of the month of August

About
the
Month
of

August

"August," from the *Brevarium Grimani* by Simon Bening (c.1510)

August: The Eighth Month

In the parching August wind,
Cornfields bow the head,
Sheltered in round valley depths,
On low hills outspread.
   — *"A Year's Windfalls," Christina G. Rossetti*

In ancient Rome, the month we know as August was originally known as *Sextilis*, meaning sixth. That's because the Roman calendar of the time had March as the first month of the year. It originally had only 29 days, but in his great calendar reform in 45 BCE, Julius Caesar added two days to the month. In 8 BCE, the month was renamed August in honor of Augustus, first emperor of Rome.

It's often claimed that Augustus stole one of February's days to add to his month, but the month already had 31 days long before Augustus became emperor. Augustus chose the month because it was the time of year in which he had accomplished some of his greatest triumphs, including the conquest of Egypt.

In both the Julian and Gregorian calendars, August is the eighth month of the year. It's one of seven months that have 31 days. During leap years, August and February start on the same day of the week; in non-leap years years, no month begins on the same day of the week as August. However, August and November always end on the same day of the week, regardless of the type of year.

In the Northern Hemisphere, August is a summer month, and in many European countries, the holiday month for most workers. In the Southern Hemisphere, August is the equivalent to February, deep in winter. No matter which hemisphere, August is a good month to spot a meteor; the Perseid Meteor Shower always takes place during the month.

August is also the month in the US that has the highest birthrate.

August in Other Cultures

The month of August has different names in different languages. Some nations use calendars other than the Gregorian, and their months may overlap with June. In lunar-based calendars, such as Islam, months move through the seasons. Still, many languages often have a word for August itself.

Albanian: Gusht

Arabic (Egypt, Sudan, Yemen): يونأغسطس (Aġustus)

Arabic (Levant): حزيراآب ('āb)

Arabic (Libya): الصهانيبال (hānībāl)

Arabic (Algeria and Tunisia): جوأوت (Ūt)

Arabic (Morocco): غشت (ġušt)

Azerbaijani: Avqust

Basque: Abuztu

Chinese: 八月 (Cantonese: baatyuht; Mandarin: bāyuè; Taiwanese: peh-goeh)

Croatian: Kolovoz

Czech: Srpen

Finnish: Elokuu

French: Août

German (Swiss): Auguscht (in other German dialects, it's just "August.")

Greek: Αύγουστος (Aúgoustos)

Hebrew: יואוגוסט (âvgûst)

Hindi: अगस्त (agast)

Hungarian: Augusztus

Irish (Gaelic): Lúnasa mí Lúnasa

Italian: Agosto

Japanese (traditional calendar): 九月 (kugatsu), 長月 (nagatsuki)

Korean: 팔월 (palweol)

Lithuanian: Rugpjūtis

Maori: Hereturikōkā

Old English: Wēodmōnaþ

Polish: Sierpień

Russian: август (Avgust)

Sesotho: Phato

Spanish and Portuguese: Agosto

Swahili: Agosti

Thai: Singhakhom

Vietnamese: 腉修 (tháng tám)

Welsh: Awst

Yiddish: אויגוסט (oygust)

Zulu: uAgasti

August Sayings and Superstitions

Here are some sayings and superstitions associated with the month of August.

General Supersitions

"Agosto, mês do desgosto," or "August, the month of sorrow and grief." (Brazil)

"If a cold August follows a hot July / It foretells a winter hard and dry." (Farming)

If thunderstorms occur in early August, they will continue for the rest of the month.

Don't sail on the second Monday in August, because it was the day the ancient kingdoms of Sodom and Gomorrah were destroyed. (Old seafaring superstition)

If you bathe at midnight on August 1 (Lammas Day) in Lockmaur, Sutherlandshire, you'll be cured of all bodily ailments, but you're expected to repay the Spirit of the Lake with coin. (Scotland)

Wedding Supersitions

"August, better have waited." (Western Kentucky)

"An August bride will be agreeable, And practical as well."

"Married in August's heat and drowse/Lover and friend in your chosen spouse."

"Whoever wed in August be, many a change is sure to see."

The following days in August are considered auspicious for weddings: August 2, 11, 18, 20 and 30.

As for which day of the week to get married, that's easy.

Monday for health, Tuesday for wealth,
Wednesday best of all, Thursday for losses,
Friday for crosses, Saturday for no luck at all.

A Regency wedding proposal

August Symbols

Birthstone: Peridot or sardonyx.

Peridot

Sardonyx (The ancient Cup of the Ptolemies, probably made in
Alexandria, Egypt, in the 1st Century CE)

Birth Flowers: Poppy or Gladiolus, both symbolizing strength of character, love, marriage, and family.

Vase with Cornflowers and Poppies, by Vincent van Gogh

Vase with Red Gladioli, by Vincent van Gogh

"August," by Eugène Grasset

Michael Dobson

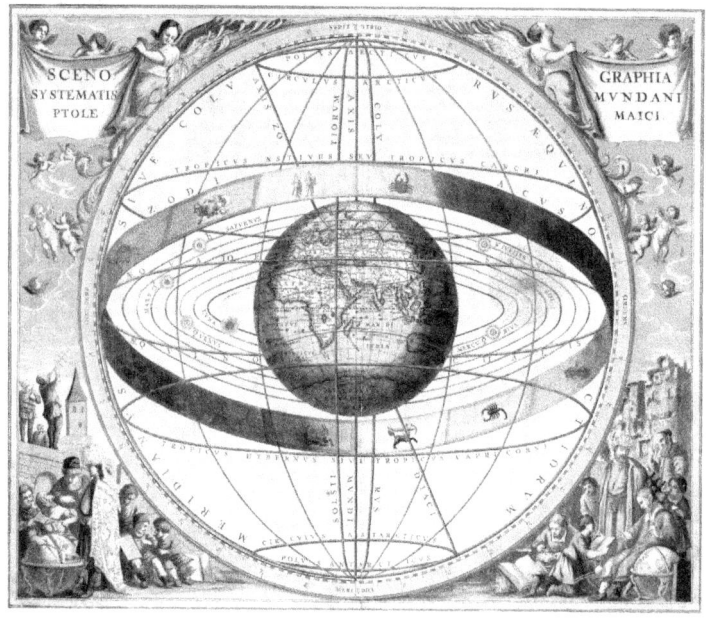

Scenography of the Ptolemaic Cosmography, by Johannes van
Loon, based on Andreas Cellarius's *Harmonia Macrocosmica,* 1660

August 12 Zodiac Signs

From the perspective of someone on Earth, the Sun appears to move through the sky throughout the year, along a path astronomers call the *ecliptic plane*. The ecliptic plane is divided into twelve constellations, known as the zodiac, based on traditionally observed patterns of stars. On your birthday, you can't see your constellation, because it's in the daytime sky.

The zodiac was first developed by Babylonian astronomers about 2,500 years ago. Because they were unaware that the Earth wobbles like a spinning top (known as *precession*), they didn't make allowance for the fact that the Sun's path through the zodiac changes over time.

That means there are now two sets of dates for your birth sign. The *tropical dates* are the original Babylonian dates; the *sidereal dates* tell you where the Sun actually appears as it moves along its annual path.

For August 12, the tropical sign is **Leo** and the sidereal sign is **Cancer**.

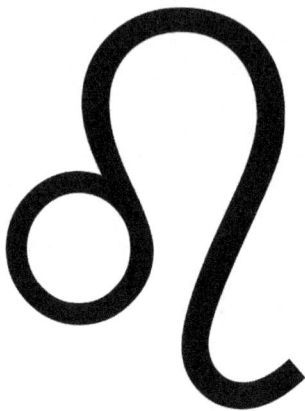

Leo

Tropical July 23 to August 22
Sidereal August 16 to September 15

Leo is one of the earliest recognizable constellations, with its stars forming a sickle or backward question mark. The Mesopotamians, the Persians, the Jews, and the Indians all had a name for the constellation that meant "lion." In Greek mythology, the Nemean lion was impervious to any weapons, but the hero Hercules nevertheless defeated it.

In astrology, Leo is a fire sign, suggesting that Leos are strong-willed and passionate. Leos are supposed to be compatible with Aquarius, Aries, and Sagittarius, but not with Gemini, Capricorn, or Pisces.

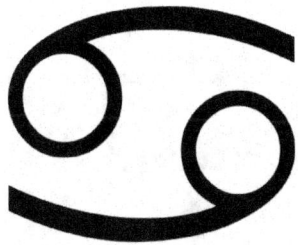

Cancer

Tropical June 21 to July 22
Sidereal July 16 to August 15

The Greek word for "crab" is Καρκινος (Karkinos), later Latinized as carcinus, which evolved into our word cancer. In Greek mythology. In one telling, when Hercules was battling the Hydra, Zeus's wife Hera sent Karkinos to distract the hero, but Hercules kicked it with such force that it was thrown into the sky, becoming a constellation. (Some say that Hercules crushed the crab with his foot and that Hera placed the crab in the night sky as a reward for its service.)

Because of the association with the disease, some astrologers refer to those born under the sign of Cancer as "moon children," because the ruling planet of Cancer is the Moon.

Cancers (or Moon Children) are supposed to be loyal, dependable, caring, and adaptable, but can also be moody, self-pitying, and oversensitive. Cancers are supposed to be particularly compatible with Scorpios, Piceans, and other Cancers.

Illustration by Edward Penfield

What Day of the Week is August 12?

On what day of the week does August 12 fall?

Surprisingly, this isn't an easy question. Because the calendar year is 365 days long (366 in leap years), it doesn't divide evenly by the seven days of the week.

Also, the Earth goes around the Sun in about 365-1/4 days, so a calendar tends to drift over time. That's why the same date falls on different weekdays in different years.

This is made even more complicated by a change in calendars that took place in 1582. Our modern calendar has its roots in ancient Rome, in a calendar reform conducted by Julius Caesar. Caesar commissioned mathematicians to attack the problem, and they came up with the idea of leap years, and thus standardized the calendar for centuries to come. This was called the Julian calendar.

Over time, however, the small errors in Caesar's calculation compounded. That's why Pope Gregory XIII commissioned the Gregorian calendar, used in most of the world today. Some countries converted in 1582, when the calendar was first developed; some converted later; other still haven't changed.

Gregorian and Julian aren't the only types of calendars. The Hebrew year, the Islamic year, and many other calendars are used in different parts of the world and among different people.

You can convert Gregorian dates to other calendars, including the Hebrew calendar, the Islamic calendar, and even the Mayan calendar by visiting the Fourmilab Calendar Converter at http://www.fourmilab.ch/documents/calendar/.

Chinese calendar systems are quite complex and have changed several times; a full discussion is far beyond the scope of this book. If you're interested, you can find information here: http://www.hermetic.ch/cal_stud/chinese_cal.htm.

On Names and Dates

Historians use "CE" (Common Era) and "BCE" (Before the Common Era) instead of the more common "AD" (Anno Domini, or Year of Our Lord) and "BC" (Before Christ), reflecting the fact that the year-numbering system established by the Gregorian calendar is used throughout the world in many countries not culturally Christian.

The CE/BCE designation dates back to at least 1708, and has been adopted as a standard by the United Nations and the Universal Postal Union. Because this series of books covers events and people of all nations and cultures, we use the CE/BCE terms.

The abbreviation "O.S." ("Old Style") on some dates refers to the fact that the Russian Empire did not switch from the Julian to the Gregorian calendar at the same time as the rest of Europe, and therefore some figures and events have two dates.

Also, in the Julian calendar in England in the 16th century, the year began on March 25 rather than January 1. To avoid confusion with Gregorian dates, dates between January and March were often written using both years.

People and events whose original names are not in the Western alphabet have their native names (where possible) in the appropriate script shown in parenthesis. If you are using an e-reader to access an electronic version of this book, all characters don't always display on all devices.

A 50-year brass perpetual calendar.

Quote of the Day

"Time is an illusion, lunchtime doubly so."

Douglas Adams,
from *The Hitchhiker's Guide to the Galaxy*

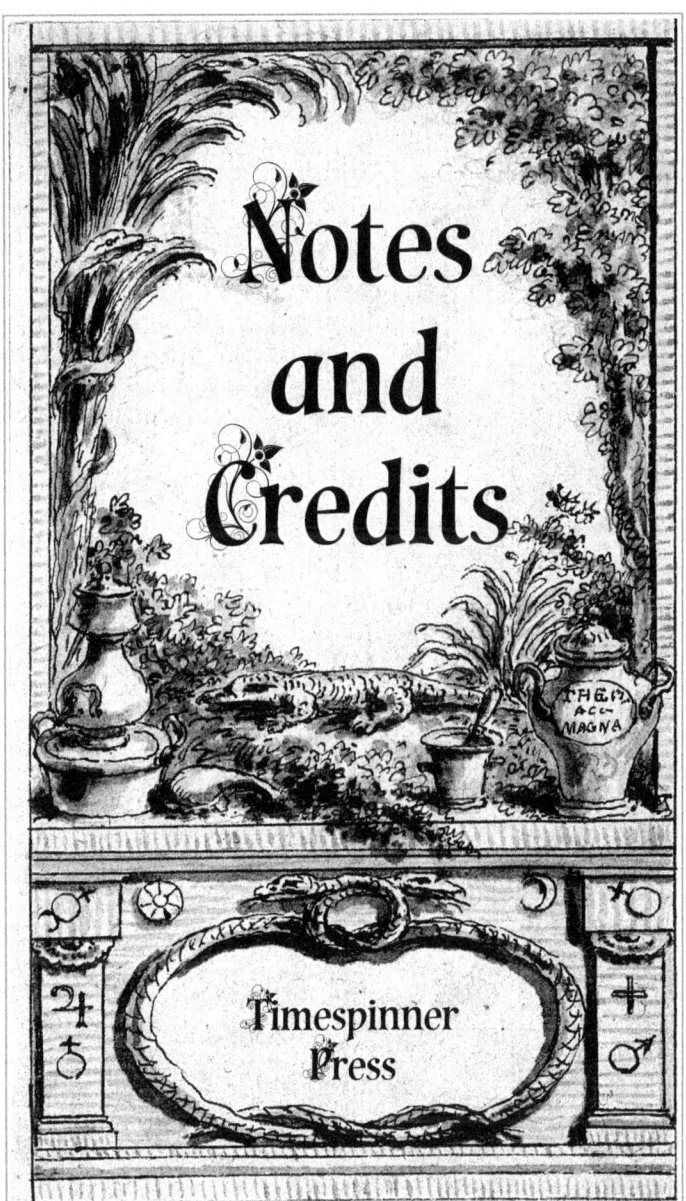

Notes
and
Credits

Timespinner
Press

Cartoon by John T. McCutcheon

Copyright, Credit, and Contact

Follow Us

Our blog "This Day in History" (http://
timespinnerpress.com/this-day-in-history/) features short
articles on events and people associated with each day, and
updates several times each week. Also subscribe to the
"Quote of the Day" at http://timespinnerpress.com/quote-
of-the-day/. You can get daily links by following us on
Facebook at TimespinnerPress, or on Twitter as
@sidewisethinker.

Contact Us

Find an error or a format problem? Want information about
the series, about us, or about when the volume for your
special day might be available? Please email us at
editor@timespinnerpress.com. (We also take requests if your
special day isn't yet complete. Please give us at least six
weeks' notice if possible.)

Sources

We owe a great debt to Wikipedia, which is our first stop for
research. We attempt to make independent confirmation of
all important dates and facts through a variety of other
sources.

Other sources we frequently use include the Library of
Congress; "on this day" listings from *Encyclopedia Britannica*,
the *New York Times*, and the BBC; Omniglot for the names of
months in other languages; *Chase's Calendar of Events*; and, of
course, the always essential Google.

All art and photographs are either in the public domain, used under a Creative Commons license, or with a "fair use" justification, and most frequently come from Wikimedia Commons and the Library of Congress Prints and Photographs Division.

Attribution is provided where possible, or as requested by the copyright owner, or when there is particular historical significance, listed below. For information about any particular illustration or photograph, please contact us.

Credits

1. The cover illustration is a detail from the 1885 painting *The Meeting of Antony and Cleopatra, 41 BC,* by Lawrence Alma-Tadema. The image is in the public domain because its copyright has expired. The original is owned by a private collector.

2. The illustration of the month of August used on the back cover is from the French Gothic illuminated manuscript *Les Très Riches Heures du duc de Berry* by the Limbourg Brothers, Jean Colombe, and an intermediate painter whose name is lost to history. It is in the public domain because its copyright has expired.

3. The box graphic used on the first page is from a 1916 pamphlet entitled "Divorce versus Democracy" authored by G. K. Chesterton, originally published in London by the Society of St. Peter and St. Paul. It is in the public domain in the US because it was published prior to 1923, and is in the public domain in all countries (including the country of origin) in which the copyright time is the author's life plus 70 years or less.

4. The graphic design for the section pages in this book is from a design originally created for a pharmacy label. It is courtesy of Wellcome Images (ICV No 11073, photo V0010813), and is used here under CC BY-SA 4.0.

5. The 2016 photograph of a bust of Cleopatra VII from the exhibit "Cleopatra and the Facination of Egypt," at the Arte

Canal, Madrid, was taken by Ángel M. Felicísimo, and is used here under CC BY-SA 2.0.

6. The illustration of Cleopatra's name in hieroglyphics was created by Pearson Scott Foresman, who released the work into the public domain.

7. The 1866 painting *Cleopatra and Caesar* by Jean-Léon Gérôme is in the public domain because its copyright has expired.

8. The 1934 publicity photograph of Claudette Colbert from the film *Cleopatra* is in the public domain because it was first published in the United States between1923 and 1977 without a copyright notice. Traditionally, publicity photographs are not copyrighted because of the way in which they are intended to be used.

9. The 1891 photograph of Sarah Bernhardt as Cleopatra was taken by Napoleon Sarony, and is in the public domain because its copyright has expired. It is used courtesy of the Theatrical Cabinet Photographs of Women (TCS2), Harvard Theatre Collection, Houghton Library, Harvard University.

10. The illustration of the Battle of Actium is from the 1883 book *Naval Battles, Ancient and Modern,* by Edward Shippen (Philadelphia: J. C. McCurdy & Co.), and is in the public domain because its copyright has expired.

11. The 2008 map of the Battle of Actium was created by "Future Perfect at Sunrise," and is used here under CC BY-SA 3.0.

12. The drawing of Cleopatra by Michelangelo Buonarroti was created prior to 1564, and is in the public domain because its copyright has expired.

13. The advertisement for Singer Sewing Machines dates from approximately 1900, and is in the public domain because its copyright has expired. It is courtesy digital collections of Miami University.

14. The 1870 photograph of a quagga at the Regent's Park Zoo, London, was taken by Frederick York. It is courtesy Biodiversity Heritage Library, image number 28201475.

15. The 2010 photograph of an IBM Personal Computer model 5150 was taken by Ruben de Rijcke and is used here under CC BY-SA 3.0.

16. The photograph from *To Have and Have Not* was originally published in the January 1945 issue of *Screenland* (Liberty

Publishing). It is in the public domain because it was published in the United States between 1923 and 1963 and although there may or may not have been a copyright notice, the copyright was not renewed.

17. The painting of Nicholas II and his son Grand Duke Alexis of Russia is from the book *The Great War* (Philadelphia: G. Barrie's Sons), first published in 1915. It is in the public domain because its copyright has expired.

18. The 1970 publicity photograph from *Hee Haw* is in the public domain because it was first published in the United States between1923 and 1977 without a copyright notice. Traditionally, publicity photographs are not copyrighted because of the way in which they are intended to be used.

19. The 1912 photograph of Christy Mathewson was taken by Charles Martin Conlon. It is in the public domain because its copyright has expired.

20. The copyright status of the poster for the 1942 film *Los Tres Mosqueteros* is uncertain. If it is copyrighted, its use here is under "free use" provisions of the copyright code. The use of the image is to illustrate a historically significant person, no free alternatives exist, and the image is printed in too low a resolution to be suitable for the production of counterfeit goods.

21. The 1968 publicity photograph from *Star Trek* is in the public domain because it was first published in the United States between1923 and 1977 without a copyright notice. Traditionally, publicity photographs are not copyrighted because of the way in which they are intended to be used.

22. The glass side from the 1918 film *We Can't Have Everything* is in the public domain because its copyright has expired.

23. The illustration of Matthew Hopkins is courtesy Wellcome Images, photo number L0000812, and is used here under CC BY-SA 4.0.

24. The 1802 self-portrait by William Blake is in the public domain because its copyright has expired.

25. The 1988 photograph of John Cage was taken by Rob Bogaerts. It is from the Anefo photo collection in the Dutch National Archives, and is used here under CC BY-SA 3.0 Netherlands.

26. The 1900 photograph of Anna Held is in the public domain. It is courtesy Library of Congress Prints and Photographs Division, digital ID cph.3a23126.

27. The painting "August" from *Labors of the Months* by Simon Bening was created in the first half of the 16th century, and is in the public domain because its copyright has expired.

28. The 1898 painting *The Grouse Shoot* by Heywood Hardy is in the public domain because its copyright has expired.

29. The woodblock of a catfish by Utagawa Kuniyoshi was created prior to 1861, and is in the public domain because its copyright has expired.

30. The 1943 photograph of a Buffalo, New York, nursery school for children of working mothers was taken by Marjory Collins for the Office of War Information. It is in the public domain as a work created by an employee of the US federal government. The original photo is in the collection of the Library of Congress, digital ID fsa.8d18633.

31. The illustration of a milkman is by Gottfired Mind, and was created prior to 1814. It is in the public domain because its copyright has expired.

32. The painting "August" by Joachim von Sandrart was created prior to 1688, and is in the public domain because its copyright has expired. The original can be found in the Staatsgalerie im Schlossanlage Schleißheim, Munich, Germany.

33. The painting "August" is from the *Brevarium Grimani*, circa 1510, and is in the public domain because its copyright has expired.

34. The 1815 woodcut of a proposal is in the public domain because its copyright has expired.

35. The photograph of an emerald cut peridot was taken by Michelle Jo, who released it into the public domain in 2009.

36. The photograph of the Cup of the Ptolemies was taken by "Clio20" and is used here under CC BY-SA 3.0. The cup is in the collection of the Bibliothèque Nationale de France.

37. The 1886 paintings *Vase with Cornflowers and Poppies* by Vincent van Gogh are in the public domain because its copyright has expired.

Timespinner
Press

License Description and Terms

Aside from material purely in the public domain, photographs and other material in this book are used under specific licenses permitting free use, usually with an attribution requirement. For full text and terms of these licenses, click or enter the appropriate links below. If you believe there is an error in the copyright status or attribution of any of these images, please email us.

- Creative Commons Attribution 2.0 Generic (CC-BY 2.0): http://creativecommons.org/licenses/by/2.0/deed.en
- Creative Commons Attribution-Share Alike 3.0 Generic (CC-BY-SA 3.0): http://creativecommons.org/licenses/by-sa/3.0/
- Creative Commons Attribution-Share Alike 2.5 Generic (CC-BY-SA 2.5): http://creativecommons.org/licenses/by-sa/2.5/deed.en
- Creative Commons Attribution-Share Alike 2.0 Generic (CC-BY-SA 2.0): http://creativecommons.org/licenses/by/2.0/deed.en
- Creative Commons Attribution-Share Alike 1.0 Generic (CC-BY-SA 1.0): http://creativecommons.org/licenses/by-sa/1.0/deed.en
- CC0 1.0 Universal (CC0 1.0) Public Domain Dedication (CC0 1.0) http://creativecommons.org/publicdomain/zero/1.0/deed.en
- GNU Free Documentation License (GFDL): http://en.wikipedia.org/wiki/Wikipedia:Text_of_the_GNU_Free_Documentation_License
- License Art Libre (Free Art License): http://artlibre.org

"Août" (August) by George Auriol

Other Books from Timespinner Press

The Story of a Special Day
Michael Dobson

A series of (eventually) 366 volumes covering everything that happened on your special day! Events, births, deaths, quotes, holidays, and much more. It's like a birthday card they'll never throw away!

US$7.95 print / US$2.99 ebook.

From Plassey to Pakistan
Humayun Mirza

The history of British Colonial India and the formation of Pakistan from the unique perspective of the son of Pakistan's first president and last of the royal line of Bengal, Bihar, and Orissa! This unique historical document tells the inside story of this distinguished family, including the detailed story of the coup that toppled his father from power!

US$27.95 print

A Whole New Navy: America's War in the Pacific

Miles Durr

The most comprehensive and detailed description of America's naval war in the Pacific ever—every battle, every ship, every task force and every task group from Pearl Harbor through the Japanese surrender! A must-have for the collection of every World War II buff!

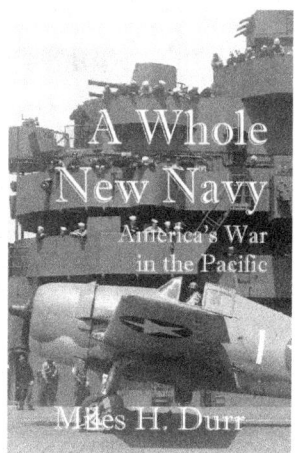

US$29.95 print

Improbable History: The Weird, the Obscure, and the Strangely Important

edited by Michael Dobson

From the birth of Western civilization to the rescue of Apollo 13, from the Leaning Tower of Pisa to Florence's Duomo, history has often turned on small, improbable details. Whatever happened to the ancient Samaritan people? Why did a fortuitous rainstorm allow the British to conquer India? How did an air raid in Italy lead to the development of chemotherapy? What happened when Albert Einstein met Adolf Hitler on the streets of Berlin? How did the Japanese manage to attack the US mainland using balloons? A cast of award-winning writers tackle some of the strangest tales in history!

US$19.95 print